Fret Not
MY CHILD

An inspirational poetry collection
by Yolanda McElroy

MoChaPrism

www.mochaprism.com

Fret Not My Child
An inspirational poetry collection
by Yolanda McElroy

ISBN: 978-1-951288-04-4 (eBook)
ISBN: 978-1-951288-05-1 (paperback)
ISBN: 978-1-951288-06-8 (hardcover)

Published by MochaPrism, LLC
Columbus, Ohio
www.mochaprism.com

Table of Contents

Dedication 5

Be Strengthened 6

If You Just Believe 7

Create Life 8

Soon Coming Return 9

Morning Prayer 10

Faithfulness 10

Spirit of The Lord 11

Look for That Day 12

Your Kingdom 14

To Know My Kingdom 15

Created By the Spirit of God 16

Rest, My Child 17

Your People 18

Still Waters 20

Peace 21

Upon This Rock 22

...Just Believe 23

For the Love of God 25

Ask 26

Fret Not My Child 27

I Love You 28

To You 29

Kudos 30

The Gift 31

Extensions... 33

Look to The Heavenlies 34

Don't You Want to Go 35

I'm An Overcomer 36
My Mountain Mover...37
Gentle Kindness..38
God Believes in You 39
Encourage Yourself...40
Beyond Words...41
As You Chose 42
Rest..43
Source Code 43
Go Forth 44
Turning Point..45
Father, To Child 46
Silent Return of Strength..47
Gather Hope..48
Hope Changes the Situation...................................49
God Sends a Comforter...50
So Quickly 51
These Things Come by Faith...................................52
Until Strongholds Are Destroyed 53
Word of Victory...54
About the Author 57
About the Designer 58

Dear Reader:

Be encouraged. There is a God who hears, who understands. If you feel you can't talk to anyone, cry out to Him. He'll understand. He'll hold your hand.

This my journal, my cry to Him. When these poems were written, I couldn't always see that He was answering me. But as I looked back over time, I recognized His still, small voice was always there, speaking to my heart – telling me to *Fret Not My Child*. May you find encouragement in these same words.

Be Strengthened

I have ordained your strength.
Even this day, I have commanded it to be.
I who made the heavens,
Shall be that strength in thee.
I have ordained your strength.
No longer shall you be weak.
But as you seek my face, you'll understand
That I have placed boldness within thee.
Glorify my name.
Give my due honor for always.
In confidence, worship and adore me,
And offer to me praise.
I have given you strength.
I have given you authority.
Use the power of my words,
And take dominion over the enemy.
Satan has been cast down.
His reign over you has ended,
through the power of Jesus Christ.
Know this, and take strength.
Praise me in boldness
And freely give me your life,
Knowing that the love of Christ
Shall sustain you
In power and in strength.

If You Just Believe

Believe in the word
That I've given into your heart.
Draw strength as you recall
The things I've said.
Be confident, be confident
In what I've said I'd do.
Know that I shall never leave
my own.
You are my child.
You belong to me.
I created you to share in my glory.
You are my child,
So come to me and ask,
And believe that I will help
my own.
Be strong in me.
Be free forever.
No longer bound by the fears
That I have loosed you from.
My child, be strong
And chose to believe
on me.

Create Life

When words are all that's left,
Then use the words to create life;
Speak the will of God into existence
Then by faith, wait until it comes.
Reach inside the spirit
Which God has given to you,
Reach with all your might
To grasp that essence
Of life in Christ.
Know that he will supply
The needed talent and desire
That you might work for his glory.

Soon Coming Return

By his Holy Spirit, our Savior says
Soon, shall I make my return.
Within the heart, he speaks to man
Prepare, for I shall soon come.
Can't you tell that my coming's near?
I give you many signs
Murder, rape, abuse and crime
All signs of ending times
Sodom and Gomorrah
A land of sin, upon which
I let my judgment rain.
Prepare, for I am coming soon
To judge the earth again.
I give you warning
I pray you heed
For what more can I do?
I already sent my precious Son,
Messiah, to die for you.
So now prepare, and turn to me
That my mercies you might know
For soon, the final trump shall sound
And to eternal life shall
Only my people go.

Morning Prayer

All that I am,
all that I ever shall be,
blessed redeemer God,
have mercy on me.

Faithfulness

Faithfulness
Is in my Spirit
Is to be prayed for,
Then received
I shan't deny that type of request
For in asking for faithfulness,
You're asking for me.

Spirit of The Lord

In the Word my Lord did say
he'd send a comforter my way
One who'd abide forever with me
Holy
Spirit of the Lord
who upon my heart has poured
the anointing of his presence
that purifies my mind and soul
Holy, holy
is your precious Spirit, Lord
Spirit of Jesus Christ
that bears witness to your children
that we are borne of God most high
Holy, holy
Spirit that is nigh and free
to those who call on you
giving us the strength forever
to do your will

Look for That Day

Are you looking for the day
when I shall make my return,
when I shall come to gather my own?
Are you looking forward to that day,
praying that it be soon
that I make my return in glory?
Are you ready?
Are you ready for the judgment
which shall be based upon my Word,
the Word which I pleaded that all
should heed?
Are you ready?
Are you ready to meet me face to face,
confident I'll show you mercy in
acknowledging you,
because I knew from day to day
you weren't ashamed to trust me?
Are you ready?
Are you ready?
Are you ready.

Prepare, prepare, prepare.
If you're not ready, pray and beware.
Watch, for that day shall soon come.

The times, the seasons, are full of my signs.
Look, understand, and hear.
Know that you must prepare,
for my coming is near, so near.
Trust me, believe me,
give me your hand.
I more than gladly will help you.
By my Spirit you can prepare,
that you might be ready
when I return.

Without my strength, there is no way
you could ever stay in my paths.
But know I love you, and will do
what is needed to help you through
if you confess my name, trust and obey,
take strength, and ask of me.
For the days are passing quickly
and soon, so soon, I'll come.

Your Kingdom

What is it like in your kingdom?
What is it like up there?
Where angels move at your command,
seeking to do your will.
Where the power of sin is broken,
destroyed, never to rise again.
What is it like up there?
What is it like to abide in a perfect kingdom,
where peace is for all to have?
Where love is in abundance,
and joy always abounds?
What is it like
to rejoice continually in you,
and to ever give you praise?
Holy, holy, holy - forever to be on my lips?
What is it like
to forget about sickness, disease, and death,
to remember that by you the curse is destroyed?
What is it like in your kingdom, Lord?
What is it like up there?

To Know My Kingdom

If you want to know what my kingdom is like,
search the Word, I'll help you understand.
Pray by my Spirit, and seek for wisdom;
for my Spirit knows my mysteries -
and can reveal those truths to you.
If you want to know what my kingdom is like,
serve and seek after me
that one day I may show you
exactly what my kingdom is like.

Created
By the Spirit of God

In the Spirit
God looks at me
and by the Spirit
sees what I can't see
substance of something
that is there
which has yet to materialize.
In the Spirit it is real
yet in the natural
I can't yet feel
nor touch it with my hand
but in the Spirit
it does stand.

In the Spirit
God created me
and by his Word
caused me to be
breathing into me
his precious gift of life
Though in the natural

things appear unclear
yet by his love, I shall not fear
for it is Christ who causes me to understand
that by his Spirit within my spirit
soon strong in him I'll stand.

Rest, My Child

Rest, my child
rest in me
for I give peace
and liberty.
Put down your cares
and seek my face
and in me find mercy
and abundant grace.
Forget your worries
and call my name,
believe on me
and you shall be changed.
Believe, trust
and come to me,
for I died my child
to make you free.
Rest, rest

and lean on me,
you shall not fall
for I am he who died to give you life.
Look to me, my child
and take your rest,
not long after
you shall be blessed.
Rest, my child
and believe on me.

Your People

Your people
your people
the souls of your people
lying injured in the street,
Lord Jesus please help me
to stretch out my hands
and minister to the need
of the souls of your people
lying injured, in the street.
The souls of your people
Lord, I see as I pass by
injured, in the street
preparing to die,

But Lord Jesus let me stop
and not casually pass by
ignoring the souls of your people
your people
lying injured in the street,
preparing to die
and 'haps hell for to meet,
But help me Lord Jesus
to go quickly to their side
and from their pain and injuries
help me not to hide,
But through the love of Jesus
Lord, help me strong to stand
and minister to the souls of your people,
your people
lying injured in the street
preparing to die
and 'haps hell for to meet,
But Lord Jesus, help me
minister to the need
and with your Word which restores life
their wounded spirits feed
that the souls of your people
would no longer lie
injured in the street.

Still Waters

Be still, my child
and hear the words of my heart
Be still, my child
and hear the words of your God
Take time, and worship me
and I will be near to you
Take time to love me
and I'll hold your requests so dear
Be still, my child
and you shall find release,
From everyday worries
I shall give you sweet peace
Cast your cares upon me
and I will carry you through
As you are still, my child
I shall speak to you
Glorify my name
Worship and give me glory
Be still and take time
to appreciate how far I've brought you
Be still in me, and trust that
further I'll lead you
As you're still, as you're still
As you're still in your heart
Listening for me.

Peace

Peace I give to you
Peace I leave with you
Let your heart abide in me
and let not worries or petty cares
fill your soul.
Peace I give to you
My peace I leave with you
Let my love fill
the empty part of your heart
that your life might be lived in joy
that your strength might be of me
Peace I give to you,
eternally.

Upon This Rock

The gates of hell shall not prevail
but it shall be as God has spoken.
By the power of the Lord in Christ
the curse of sin is broken.
No longer hold your head down in shame,
but know that you have been made free.
As you receive the truth of Jesus into your heart,
sin shall not overcome thee.

We're more than conquerors
through Jesus, who loves us.
We're more than mighty,
as we submit, to God most holy;
And the gates of hell shall not prevail over us,
for we give to God glory.
And the gates of hell shall not prevail over us,
for in Jesus we trust.
And we know, that greater is our God
who fights for us.

...Just Believe

I love you more
than you could ever know
I love you more
than you could ever know
I love you
You're my child
You belong to me
Trust me as I guide you
into truth, liberty
Oh, my child, I love you
seek and believe on me!

For the Love of God

For the love of God
is shed abroad
in my heart.
And I shall follow him
forever
and seek his will.
Because it is God
who worketh in me, perfecting desire
to trust in him, and to believe on his power.

By the grace of God
I shall endure
until the end.
By his holiness
I shall live
free from sin.
Because it is he
who is
the author and the finisher of my faith
and through him
I shall live and overcome,
by his grace.

I shall claim my victory, walk in authority
for in the name of Jesus
I have been made free
because greater is my Lord
greater is my Lord
greater is my Lord Jesus
who perfecteth me.

The Lord shall perfect
The Lord shall perfect
The Lord shall perfect
that which concerneth me
The Lord shall perfect
The Lord shall perfect
The Lord shall perfect
that which concerneth you

For when he begins
a good work
inside your heart
he shall perform it
until the day of his return

Ask...

I've been asking the Lord for a special love
A love that forever abides,
A love that starts within my heart
And in my spirit hides.
I've been asking the Lord for a special love
One that's forever pure,
And regardless of the tests and trials,
One which will always endure.
I've been asking the Lord for a special love
A love that's truly real,
A love based on the facts in God
Not based on how I feel.
I've been asking the Lord for a special love
A love in which I'm free,
To live and be exactly who
My God desires me be.
I've been asking the Lord for a special love
A love in which I'll stand,
Confident knowing my Savior's there
And that my God does hold my hand.
I've been asking the Lord for this special love
Where Jesus is always my King,
A love which strengthens me in knowing
Through Christ I can do all things.

Fret Not My Child

Fret not my child
for I am near thee
I have healed
and delivered thee
Continue to seek hard
after me
and I will receive you to glory
Fret not my child
for I have given you rest
Abide in my Spirit
and be ye blessed
Trust and believe in what I say
and walk uprightly in my way
Fret not my child
for I am your guide
I will lead you
in paths upright
So follow me, trust and obey
and in my Word forever stay
Fret not my child
for I love you
Believe that I have brought you through.
Believe that I have answered your call.
Believe, and you shall never fall.

I Love You

Lord, how can my attitude be changed
so that I'm always in the mood
to give you thanks, and honor, and glory
...because you've done much more for me
than many could ever realize.
When I cried all night long
with a pillow smothering my sorrow,
you dried the tears, and wiped the
sadness from my eyes.
When I wanted to die, because I felt
my life wasn't worth living,
you spoke to my heart the words "I love you".
You called me your own
when I believed there was no way possible
I could still belong to you.
Rather, I thought, because of my actions,
you'd condemn me too.
...But you didn't
You just kept saying
"I love you."

To You

Child, I love you
my child, I love you
forever and always
Just humbly seek after me
and I will help you stay
in my paths, in my light, under my wing
caring that you're safe from harm
Know that I love you
and my ways
my ways are peace
Trust, believe, seek after me
and I will help you see
through the love I have for you
that I am your provider and your king
Come to me, my child
and ask for any good thing
Believe I love you
and I hear your cries at night
Believe I love you enough
to dry your tears
through the love I have for you
eternally, through grace
eternally. My child
my child, I love you.

Kudos

You made a mighty sacrifice for me.
Perfection stood in place of my imperfection.
Joy took on my sorrow.
Hope took on my despair.
You allowed your heart to break
to provide that mine would be healed.
You gave so much for me...
I know I don't completely understand,
but I'd like to thank you.
I pray that such a degree of love
might well up in my heart for you;
that for you I'd gladly alter my ways -
as long as I could walk closer to you.
You sacrificed your life to please the Father,
and in doing so, you saved mine.
Thank you.
I recognize that true power
is not so much in the words I say,
but in the actions which follow...
I pray that by your grace
with joy, a changed lifestyle
within me might come.

The Gift

I may not have a million
to lay before your feet
Nor the voice of a lark
to offer songs so sweet
I may not have the skill
to build you a temple with my hands
But that which I have, I bring to you
to be used as you command.
I bring you the gift of love,
out of gratitude for Christ above.
I may not know all your ways
which are more perfect than mine
Or have answered your call
immediately each time
But today and now
I give you praise
for Jesus you are special to me
and by your grace working in my heart
I am becoming holy
By the strength of your love
you reached out your hand
and demanded hell and earth
to lose their command
to release their grip, their hold on me

and with the gift of your life
in you I am free.
But what have I to give in return?
A gift that comes from the heart
surely you would not spurn
So my Lord these words I bring to you
for by your grace
my love for you
is starting to come through.

Diamonds and gold I never wanted,
your love is much more precious to me.
I own all the material things,
but your love and your heart you must offer to me.

Extensions ...

I shall lift up my hands
and reach for my Lord
through praise.
I shall cry out to him
when I cry out in prayer,
knowing my God hears.
My God is a reachable God;
He's one who's very near.
And if I ever need to lean on his strength
I know I can, for he cares.
I can reach the heavens
when I reach with my heart,
my mind, my spirit, and my soul.
When I cry for understanding,
then God shall bless me
and allow me his pathways to know.
For my God is a reachable God,
who wants to be close to me.
So I shall lift up my hands
And reach for my Lord
through praise.
And cry out to him
when I cry out in prayer,
that he might bless me

with understanding and grace
and strength to stretch with all my heart
for my very reachable God.

Look to The Heavenlies

Look to the heavenlies
where the Father abides
Look to the love I've given you
through Jesus Christ
Trust, believe, hold on
to what I've said before
Remember what I've told you
it's faith which opens the door
So have faith my child, have faith,
and look unto me
With your heart, your mind, your spirit
Look to the heavenlies.

Don't You Want to Go?

Don't you want to go
when I come
for my people
Israel?
Don't you want to go
and rule with me
and in my presence dwell?
Don't you want to go
when I call nations into my rest?
Don't you want to go with me
and forever be blessed?
Don't you want to go
and see the beauty of my temple,
the perfectness of my peace,
and the purity of my love?
Don't you want to go
and forever stay with me?
I'm calling you to seek after me,
to search out my ways.
I'm calling you to pray to me,
to be aware of the passing days.
I'm calling you to trust in me,

to let your love grow -
so that you can go with me
and my pathways you can know.
Don't you want to go with me
to a place where pain is no more?
Don't you want to go with me
and live forever more?

I'm An Overcomer

Why should I give up now
when I've been promised victory?
Why should I hold sadness in my heart
and accept the lie of defeat?
For Jesus, the truth, the way, and the life
promised to walk by my side.
He promised never to leave or forsake me,
he promised to be my guide.
There's no way I shall embrace defeat
when I know that God embraces me.
Christ Jesus didn't tuck tail and run
and I shan't either, for he's a part of me.

My Mountain Mover

Though the tears may fall
and through it all
I don't completely understand,
I look to you Jesus
for your Word says
you shall help me stand.
Though the enemy comes
in a flood of lies
trying to make me doubt,
yet will I trust in you Jesus
for you promised to work it out.
When all around
seems chaos and despair,
I glorify you Jesus
for yet are you there.
You still have the power
you still have the might,
so I'll stand still in your promises
and with your Word fight.
You have given me your Spirit
you have given me your hand,
so through the power of you Jesus
mountain move at this command.
These trials shall soon be over

for they are not mightier than you,
for all these reasons, and simply for your grace
Lord Jesus I magnify you.

Gentle Kindness

In the eyes of the Almighty
I have found mercy
In the eyes of my Creator
I have found love
In his gentle kindness
my Savior looked from the heavens
In His eyes I have found favor
Favor from God above

God Believes in You

Believe in the Lord who believes in you
Trust in the God who wants oh to trust you
Hold to the hand of he who carries you,
carries you through the storms of life.
Call on he who calls you day by day
Seek to him to know the lightened pathway
Take up his cross, for he laid down his life
to bring you rest
Trust in God
Trust in God
Trust in his name.

Encourage Yourself

...and David encouraged himself in the Lord.
And David encouraged HIMSELF in the Lord.
No one encouraged him,
but David encouraged himself.
He didn't seek his own strength,
but he sought the strength of God.
...and David encouraged himself IN THE LORD.
He sought encouragement in the
Lord who created him,
who called his life into being.
...and David ENCOURAGED, not belittled or
condemned, but encouraged himself in the Lord.
I can do all things through Christ which strengtheneth
me. Greater is he that is in me
than he that is in the world.
...and David encouraged himself in the Lord.
David enCOURAGED himself in the Lord,
built up his spirit in strength, by thinking
on the name of his God.
They that wait upon the Lord shall
renew their strength.
Be strong in the Lord and in the power of his might.
...and David encouraged himself in the Lord.
Encourage YOURSELF in the Lord.

Beyond Words

Don't let words get in the way
accusations and excuses
agitations and attitudes
Don't let them distract you,
for they are not of me.
Don't let words get in the way,
but by my Spirit
stretch before me,
trusting me to send my anointing
to break every yoke that hinders.
As you praise me, I will move.
As you glorify me, I will bless.
As you exalt my name, and my name alone,
then shall you understand, then shall you realize,
that only by my power does freedom come...
So praise me, praise me
allow me to be glorified in your heart,
for I am the Lord Almighty,
and I alone am worthy of all praise.

As You Chose

As you chose
help me go
As you teach
help me know
As you strengthen
help me grow
that I might be of use to you
Bless me talk
as you talk
Help me walk
as you walk
continually seeking your face
And forever bless me to hope
eternally for your grace
as you help me Lord Jesus
to yield and do
exactly as you chose.

Rest

Rest, my child
and abide in me
have faith and believe
that I will keep you
by my power
through mercy and grace.
Rest, my child
and trust in me.

Source Code

Discouragement comes from the world
but encouragement comes from God's Word.
Strength to endure comes in knowing
your prayers in Christ are heard.

Go Forth

Go forth anyway
when it seems
as if there's no day
for God has commanded
your deliverance
so trust him and obey.
Through the fire walk;
Go forth anyway.
Go forth anyway
when the flames appear to roar
knowing Jesus is your stay
and through him you can endure;
Go forth anyway.
Go forth, go forth, go forth
be strong
knowing all along
that through Jesus you shall
come through,
for much greater than he
that is in the world
is he that dwells within you.

Turning Point

When the storms seem
to roar
and billows appear
to roll,
I turn to you Jesus
for you keep my soul.
When the enemy tries
to assail me
and tempt me to sin,
I turn to you Jesus
for you dwell within.
It's your arms that uphold me
your love that's so true,
so when I feel I can't go on
Jesus I turn to you.
For you are a mighty redeemer
possessing abundant strength,
you are a gentle leader
who would go to any length
to keep those who call on you
in your safely guarded ways,
that we might ever turn to you
and forever give you praise.

Father, To Child

Daughter, you are dear to me
I hear the words you say
I speak through them to let you know
that I am near
I am your comfort.
I am your God.
Seek me more, and you shall have
the closeness with me that you desire.
When you draw close to me,
then I draw close to you.
Continue seeking, and you shall have
the closeness you desire.
Call upon my name
that I might help you understand my Word.
Call upon my Spirit
to lead and guide you in all truth.
Be steadfast, my daughter
and study to know that I have
created you new.
I have done a new thing in your life
so that you would come to me in love.
Love me with all your heart,
then my commandments shall not
be burdensome.

Trust in me, then the
self-condemnation shall pass.
Hope in my Word, and you
shall never be ashamed.
Study and pray, my daughter,
then you shall know.
My return is drawing closer,
so draw closer to me, my child.
As I purify your heart, mind, and soul
through the spirit of my Word.

Silent Return of Strength

You grow stronger
day by day
as you meditate upon my Word,
and seek my strength through prayer.
Samson wasn't aware
that my strength was returning
to him, yet it was.
Believe in faith
that your strength in me
has come.

Gather Hope

Gather hope for one more day
Gather hope for one more day
Believing Jesus shall make a way.
Take his Word into your heart,
and stand in faith.
Gather hope for one more day
Gather hope for one more day
Ever giving God the praise.
For he knows how to keep his own,
to keep his own, through faith.
Hope in God's Word.
Hope in God's strength.
Hope in God's promises.
Believe upon his name.
When the night seems
to overcome your day,
gather hope in God's Word
and stand, by faith.

Hope Changes the Situation

Hope, hope
in the Word of God.
Hope, hope
in Jesus name.
Hope, hope
in his promises.
If you hold to hope,
you shall be changed.
Hope in the things
that your eyes can't see.
Believe God for your victory.
Hope, and you shan't be ashamed.
Hope, forever, in Jesus name.

God Sends
A Comforter

Receive comfort from the Lord, your God.
Know that even now, he is there with you.
Know that he has heard your cry, and even now
is come to heal you.
Glorify the Lord who gives you life.
Know that he shall multiply your peace as you
learn of him. Call upon his Spirit
to heal your mind and to help you
with emotions that you cannot yet control.
Seek God - he will answer. He will answer.
He dries the tears, and prevents
them from falling. Seek to know the voice
of the Lord God, who speaks to you.
Know he loves you so....Be strengthened.
God will surely keep you. Focus on the power of his
name. Know, even now, God is for you.
Even now, he is with you.
Call on him, for he has answered,
And surely, he has healed.

So Quickly

So quickly
So quickly
There is no more time,
and Christ shall return
so quickly.
Prepare, my children
for soon I shall return.
Don't be caught, dear children
with your work undone.
Study, to show thyself
approved unto me.
Study, dear children
for I am coming quickly.
Storms are increasing
throughout all the land.
Violence daily, against
all man.
Sickness, disease, claims
many souls.
Prepare, my children for
these are the woes
which were promised to be.
So study, dear children, and know
that I am coming so quickly.

These Things Come by Faith

By faith, by faith
these things come by faith.
Understanding, wisdom and knowledge,
receive these things by faith.
Salvation, hope of eternal life,
receive these things by faith.
Faith can move mountains,
for mountains hinder your view
of the promises of God.
By faith, command the mountains to move
By faith, expect it shall be done
Faith is the evidence of things not seen
By faith, know it shall be
By faith, Jesus cursed the fig tree
By faith in Jesus, forever be free
and take up the word of faith into your mouth
and bind the spirit of the enemy.

Until Strongholds Are Destroyed

Pray until the strongholds
are destroyed in your life.
Take up the Word of God
and pray as his Spirit leads.
Pray until anointing falls
and you know, by faith, that
a change has come.
Prayer is your communication with God.
The Word is God's communication with you.
Change will come through prayer
and the Word of God.
Stay in prayer
and study God's Word
and know that your change has come.

Word of Victory

Write my way out? How?!
How, when the thoughts
are a jumble
and my mind is racing
When my flesh is down,
and the spirit within me struggling to breathe...

I will bless the works
of your hands
I will prosper the words
of your mouth
I draw nearer to you as you write
and I reassure you, as you reassure yourself.
Don't lose sight of the prize,
the victory is already yours.
The flesh must be conquered.
Know it can be conquered through
the Spirit of Jesus Christ.
You fight in order to have victory.
Dust yourself off!
Get into the battle!
Have faith, and look to me!
I ordain your season of suffering,
and I ordain burdens to be broken.

I am Jehovah God, and I will keep you -
if you would allow it be so.
The things you desire to be changed in
your life, shall change
but only as you allow me to transform
you by my Word.
What does my Word say?
It says that you are more than a
conqueror through me.
You may sow in tears, but remember,
you shall reap with joy.
Ask me to send the spiritual morning!
Know that I hear you and that I'm there for you.
Know that my anointing shall also cover your mind,
and that your thoughts, even toward
yourself, shall soon change.
Fight your way through, my child.
Take my Spirit and go.
Go by what my Spirit says, not by how you feel.
The mind must be renewed,
so learn to decipher which thoughts
are still of the old man -
to these thoughts you need not be in bondage.
You are strong my child, because
I am strong within you.
I am strong for you.
Glorify my name,
for I am the God who carries you through.

For God so loved the world, that he gave his only begotten Son, that whosoever believeth in him should not perish, but have everlasting life. ~ John 3:16

For more encouragement and inspiration
visit my website at www.mochaprism.com

About the Author

Yolanda McElroy is a Dayton, Ohio native and a graduate of the Ohio State University. She is the owner of MochaPrism LLC and the author of *Ten Fingers Ten Toes,* a children's picture book. *Fret Not My Child* is her first inspirational poetry book.

Connect with Yolanda at:
Website: www.mochaPrism.com
Instagram: @mochaprism
Facebook: www.facebook.com/mochaprism

Also available on Amazon:

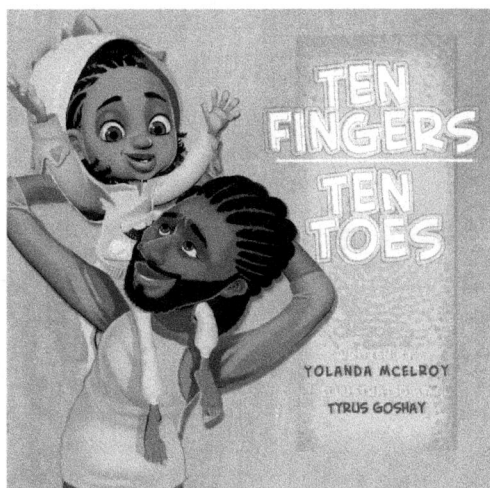

About the Designer

Celeste Payne is an artist and educator that specializes in the graphic design of books and marketing materials. She is the founder of Empowerment Sessions and produces inspirational graphics and products.

Connect with Celeste at:
Website: www.chortazoarts.com
Instagram: @empowerment4u
Facebook: www.facebook.com/chortazoarts

We hope you enjoyed this book. Please tell a friend about it & leave a review at Amazon.com.
Please also join our mailing list at www.mochaprism.com.

God bless you...

www.ingramcontent.com/pod-product-compliance
Lightning Source LLC
LaVergne TN
LVHW021625080426
835510LV00019B/2760